My Happy Place

Poetry By

Maureen Himler

"Time to Relax" was previously published in "Festival of Voices, Anthology of Poetry", The Poetry Center, 1991; "Fragile" was previously published in "Poetic Voices of America", Sparrowgrass Poetry Forum, 1991; "County Line" was previously published in "American Poetry Annual", The Amherst Society, 1991; "The Little Town of Cleveland" was previously published in "The Other Side of the Mirror", Watermark Press, 1992.

ISBN: 979-8-9878628-1-0
Maureen Himler

Library of Congress Control Number: 2023900393

ii

For everyone that has ever believed in me...

Thank you!

TABLE OF CONTENTS

PREFACE

The poetry in this book was written within a time span of 38 years — 1984 to 2022. I tend to call my younger poetic pieces my "kiddie" poems. They were written by my teenage self and tend to be more simplistic in style and tone. The styles and subject matters all vary in this book. There are references to nature, family, love, dreams, faith, society...basically, a little bit of this and a little bit of that. I do hope everyone that reads this book will be able to find at least one poem that they can connect with.

I truly hope you enjoy reading "My Happy Place"!

THE RUSH HOUR

(*THIS WAS THE FIRST POEM I EVER WROTE – FRESHMAN ENGLISH CLASS, LEJEUNE HIGH SCHOOL, CAMP LEJEUNE, NC)

At 5:00 each day,

the rush begins.

People in different cars

rushing to get home,

honking and waiting patiently.

People sitting in long lines

until it is their turn to go home,

with the MP's in the middle,

trying to get the people home safe.

So they themselves can go home and relax,

safe and sound.

FRAGILE

The sun glistens,

A cool breeze blows by,

The different bugs walk on the thin blades of grass;

The flowers bloom out in assorted colors

and the birds fly about.

How fragile would this be,

if you could hold it in your hand and squeeze?

THE LITTLE TOWN OF CLEVELAND

The little town of Cleveland

    seemed so big to me,

When I was young it looked so enormous,

    but suited me to a tee.

Now that I'm grown up,

    I go back frequently

To that little town of Cleveland,

    which seems so small to me.

THE WIND

The grass grows greener

with every step I take

The birds fly higher

as I begin the race

The sun beats down

on top of me,

The branches sway

as I pass the trees

You cannot see me,

but I am here

You breathe and feel me,

I'm everywhere.

THE FIRE

The smoke rises so very fast,

the flames holler with each blast.

They run for the door,

but it is too hot.

They go to the window,

but it is locked.

The cries of horror and defeat,

I hear from across the street;

I see a strange look in their eyes

as they move from the window;

I hear them cry.

LITERARY SPARK

One light, one single light

or spark...one single spark will do as well.

May they view it from afar

from ... a far, far distance in place.

May they also hath sense the smolder

and view the trickling of each ember

falling slowly into the abyss.

Into the abyss, where nothing ever truly lives

except for maybe Hope of finally being found.

And yet, that is where they need to go –

May they go now...send the agents down.

Do not leave anything to chance – and ignore

to where the elder's point.

The elder's eyes are old and cannot always see the truth.

May the senses guide them to the hidden one

the hidden one...who burns from inside.

THE LADY

She stands in the harbor

    waving us on,

as she did years ago...

    her special bond;

Her compassion let lay

    with the light of her torch,

many people, their lands...

    forever scorched;

Her love shines out in her

    oval-shaped eyes,

meeting the boats...

    so many goodbyes;

The tenderness and sweetness

    is shown on her face,

for the country who has given

her...everlasting grace!

THE ELDER'S EYES

The Elder's eyes are old and blue,

they have seen so much, and so much

was new.

As a child, living within other's views

his eyes grew tired of the weary news.

So, he set his sights on learning more,

seeing places and people, like never before.

Shades of blue and green mixed in with muse,

then reds and yellows flooded in by fuse.

His eyes have spent weekends in Paris.

They have trekked over to Berlin,

and seen many a lasses - in style,

smile and blush at the soldiered men.

The news photographs were a mere nothing

compared to what his eyes explored,

and many of nights, they slept teary

over the loss of those deployed.

But never a day, in his 100 years,

would his eyes concede or retreat —

His mind, is now trickling slowly out of view,

But as for the bare images —

his eyes will <u>never</u> claim defeat!

ODE TO WS

From Dover to London

    the traveler speaketh well.

Through villages and country sides

    the roads by orchards fell –

into the hearts of many, who flocked to hear his mind,

float into an echo, beneath the cathedral lights.

The crowded city

    mend his home...

Over narrow bridges,

    he hath did love.

But beyond that lied an aroma of tales,

as it was to become, his lifelong trail.

HOW WAS I NERVOUS?

How was I nervous on this rainy day?

I knew all the answers right away.

I sat at my desk and rattled them off,

one by one and not a bit tough.

Now it was over and I made my grade,

I sigh with relief as the pressure fades.

How was I nervous? I wondered that day...

I couldn't answer

I made an "A".

COUNTY LINE

My grandmother once spoke of

a place of yesteryear

where things were once simple

and life...oh so dear.

A day when love filled the room

in place of television and vcr,

as an old tuned-out radio

intervened romantic sounds...

On the border to nowhere, yet

high on the map of time,

lies a town and it's people

upon the county line.

"Across the ages and one step

over", she would say with a smile,

"The most beautiful place in

the world...My County Line".

FROM YOU TO ME

Today she thought that it would come,

the letter,

that she had been waiting on.

So, she waited and waited,

hours passed by...

yet she still sat conformed

to the porch steps of home.

Her little brown shoes

bore the wear on the soles,

from tapping all morning,

and all week on the boards.

She didn't know when, but

it will come, she would say...

to her brothers and sisters

who have teased her for days.

The sun, now it's hottest,

is beaming down on her face

and she wishes for the mail carrier

to pick up his pace.

"Is it here?" her mother peeks

out through the screen.

"No, not yet..., but it'll be here

you'll see!"

Just then, the sound of horses

could be heard from afar, and the wire

rimmed wheels dragging slowly behind...

from the clippity-clop and the neighing

she knew,

that the mailman's delivery soon

would be due.

So, she ran to the box as fast as she

could...and waited for him to bring

her good news.

The carriage stopped short,

Just an inch or two from

the little brown shoes with

the tattered old tongues.

The man opened his bag and looked

carefully through...

then turned with a smile,

"I think this is for you."

The letter addressed was in her

name alone...not her mother,

or brothers, or sisters could know...

what was inside, only she could find out,

when she opened the letter, signed

Happy Birthday...love Pop!

NEW YORK

A funny little accent

still sparks upon my lips...and through

my voice, it speaks to those

from places still too far away...too far

for them to ever know.

ON MY OWN
(DOWN BROADWAY AND BACK)

He left early that morning

his destination still unknown,

but he didn't care

for he had to find...

a place to call his own.

His feet walked for hours

down the "subs" of New York Bay,

and looking around

he wished for good...

to be lost amidst the crowd.

His stroll down Broadway

and across to 49th,

made him wonder where

or if they even cared...

"Are they looking for me tonight?"

Then shortly before bedtime

he hopped a train for home,

but he didn't care

for he had found...

a place to call his own.

If only he could explain it

to his family across the bridge,

that he made it there

down Broadway and back...

And he can make it anywhere!

LITTLE STEP BY STEP

At 28 ... He brought life into my eyes,

and love into my heart.

He showered me with questions

that I will never fully be able to answer.

He taught me how to love, without judging

and how to turn off the noisy talkers –

those who are <u>too perfect</u> to ever understand.

He and I explored Autism together,

one second at a time...

slowly learning as we went – little step by step.

We have tumbled and fallen quite a bit,

but we stood back up and started over – over and over.

He has endured all the meltdowns,

and as I have had my share as well –

we have made it out of that confusion,

by having each other –

not by listening to the noisy talkers.

At 24 … We are still learning – little step by step.

But as he continues to grow into the man

I will always love with all my heart,

he has proven that a diagnosis of Autism isn't the end…

it's just the beginning.

HOME

Two gone, and two to stay

the empty walls mark the forgotten days

when once the children would run and play

and now they run, all but to run away.

They are tired of the messy rooms,

the filthy hands, and the muddy shoes

that mother would always insist they clean

or else be gone, to bed unseen.

So now they toss and turn to grow

to escape from the noise of future growth;

where their sisters have announced to stretch about

and ride upon the shirt tails and wear them out.

Two gone, and two to stay

the empty walls fill to a circled maze;

when once not content with the rules and games

they are now quite pleased with their child's gaze.

And to where, they were not once proud to be

they grace once more with apology;

As their mother now holds their own in care,

they remember the laughter, the noise disappears.

"WHAT'S THE POINT?" AND "WHY?"

As many days seem to stand still in time, almost

creeping along their bottomless course; There are others

that pass so quickly by, that at the end of the day, you

have only to ask... "What's the point?" and "Why?".

Why must one day be filled with such a lapse, with

no or little expectations of a future to be had? Still yet,

on the other scale, there seems to be the weight, of

people filled with so much to do...in such a narrow little

space.

IF I, TO THIS DAY, HAVE EVER DOUBTED YOUR LOVE

If I, to this day, have ever doubted your love

then it is to me, by my own discourse, that I have fallen this way.

From the ashes of Timrock, to the farthest region above

I vow, to my darling, that my eyes have never meant to be locked.

For you can see, so much more clearly, than I on this stage

May my hopes become your hopes, and this fright turn away!

Little is begotten, as the acts are to be played,

but for once, I stand erect, without a seat to please my back.

"Your station, your station!" I hear the woodwinds call me home.

But to where is my station, if I have forced us to be alone?

A dearest memory, I have, and hold full thrust to the crowd,

you are my spotlight, and the lines that I fold quite tightly in vow.

For within my fingers, (Shakespeare laughs at my cold!)

I hold the most beautiful words, but will they ever be told?

CARRIE-BEAR

Once the child begins to dream,

        begins to love, and

        begins to scheme

there is no way of stopping her,

for she is what she will become.

There is no teaching to be taught,

        all is known,

        all is sought.

When life is but a measly bore,

        away she'll fly,

far away...

        she'll land;

In search of what may lie ahead,

        dreams are truth,

and truth...

        is Love.

A MOMENT

Shepherds walk across the mounds

Angels fly above the clouds

The wind rustles through the trees

The birds jolt from the branches -

taking flight in the breeze

A moment here, a moment there -

Why can't we all just stop to stare?

Take that time to swallow our pride

and enjoy the beauty that surrounds our life.

TREASURE

Treasure, where are you?

For you're neither high nor low.

Treasure, where are you?

For you're not in the autumn meadow.

I looked in the garden,

but you were not there...

I looked in the bush,

but saw you nowhere.

Treasure, where are you?

For I have to know...

If you are not with me,

I shall have to go.

SUPERFICIAL

He was lost last night and all alone

against the wind he walked,

until he fell upon his knees...

disgusted with his pride.

He loved this girl

or so his heart conceived,

and he felt so sure she did the same...

that he walked some seven miles.

Through the rain that night

his feet progressed,

half soaked to the bone...

only stopping once to greet the cold,

and then running to warm his toes.

RAINBOW DAYS

Early morning set in quite still, and as the evergreens swayed swiftly back and forth, the wind blew hard and strong.

The sun was barely able to peak through the clouds, dark and lifeless, they sat peering across the fields.

At one point, the clouds suddenly burst into buckets of rain, pouring hard and strong, as if trying desperately to compete with the wind...only to lose by a few short seconds, in the end.

By mid afternoon, only sprinkles fell. The fields, put to sleep by the storm, have now begun to awaken...standing stiffly still at first, but then gently, side by side, stretching back into place.

The clouds and the wind too, looked about the air...and seeing a sign of brighter days, took in a deep breath and shook out the rain.

"Brighter days are sure to come!" smiled the evergreens. As the clouds began to move away, the sun shot rays of colors across the fields.

IDOL

Maybe it is true –

We were never supposed to meet.

Two hearts from different worlds

shouldn't always share a space.

But somehow, we were put together

in a crazy twist of fate –

And as the music plays in the background,

I wonder if this was all but a mistake.

THE ONLY ONE

The only one I've known before

has shown to me his love through song

and through his verse,

he sings to me...and widens my perceptive scene.

The only one I've known before

could embrace so many hearts around the world

and in just a mere moment, with his smile

a glow...he can make all forget their baggaged woes.

The only one I've known before

has given hope to those with dreams

and to those whose dreams cannot fly,

he merely says...come on, let's try.

NIGHT OF ENDLESS WELLS

Pennies fall upon the snow

then melt beneath their copper coat.

Who is it that I used to be?

If only once, I'd like to see...

My faded past, blow in the wind,

my brighter future, calling me.

Nickels fall upon the sand

and then slip into a hollow land.

How is it that I used to dwell

upon a night of endless wells?

Where money only claims a few...

and others cry, they sit in pews.

For even though they fed their yearlings

a whole,

their elders sleep half empty and cold.

Dollars grow upon the trees

then fall to plant another seed.

Where is it that I used to be?

If only once, I'd like to see...

A place where people cry for joy,

a place where money is destroyed!

NUMBER ONE
(FOR JANICE)

I wasn't there for you that day,

to see your bright-eyed smiling face

when mother said, you were the first to come...

yes, the first, "You are my number one!"

And I wasn't there to take care of you,

to feed or hold...or change your clothes...

No, I wasn't anywhere to be found,

when you took your first steps

and fell to the ground.

Sometimes I wonder what might have been...

if I had been there to be the one,

who cradled you when you were sick, and

who blessed your sneezes when they wouldn't quit.

Would it have brought us closer today,

if I could have been there at an earlier age?

For you have always been there for me

when I've fell, or needed a change,

or just a hold from a friend.

But I have never been able to repay you enough...

not through presents, or favors, or life's little tucks.

So, please Sis, this poem is for you...

Number one's the greatest! And I love you!

FOR COMFORT'S SAKE

I have a sister who is a brain

and one who's smart, just not the same.

And I have another who's bold in speech...

who thinks she knows more than one could teach.

I have a sister who is of strong will

and one who pays off her husband's bills.

And one more who thinks she's too strong to be...

the baby sister of girls like these.

I have a sister who likes to tease

and one who laughs until her nose bleeds.

And I have another who tosses jokes...

faster than her mouth can quote.

I have a sister who enjoys to flirt

and one who used to look for a wedding band first.

And one more who looks, and looks some more...

but is too young to knock at love's front door.

I have a sister who lives next-door

and one who lives next to New York.

And I have another who I sometimes wish did the same...

for she lives a little too close, for my comfort's sake!

But all in all, I'd say I have the best...

three sisters I love and wouldn't want to exchange.

MERRY GO ROUND

Merry go round, merry go round

spin as fast as the wind...

with me on board,

    we'll fly away...

If only for today.

And then tomorrow,

I shall return to fly in broad

daylight...

    into the sky and clouds, I'll dream...

of my merry go round's first flight.

TWAS EVENING

Twas evening

and the night was long

too long

I feared, to walk alone.

My heart was pounding

My hands were slick

as the tears ran over

my finger's tips.

For it was here

not so long ago

too long

I forget, the name of foe

Who left her silent

Who crowned her head

as the blood ran over

the princess dead.

Twas evening

and the song was sung

so long

knelt them, by the prison's son.

They cried for shelter

They prayed for sun

as the lightning came in

the song was done.

So, it twas left

for this to be

so long

in short, a rage of greed.

Where people face

Where people lust

as only mere mortals

in search of trust.

THE CANDLEMAKER'S SONNET

If candlesticks hold the light of day

do not thou sayest, it has gone away.

The light, for which has sparked our lust

and knelt us before a kindling trust.

I have shared with no one, this light, but with you

So, then sayest with passion instead of with muse.

My embodied spirit, as with yours, it shall stay to be true.

Now speak no more into this crowded room!

For my blanket will protect us, entwined we will sleep

the knots in my shoelaces shall never hear the wind's peeps.

And bewilder not, my love, for the scent is a must rare,

the rarest of drippings, the stronger the air.

    Which shall stand between us and indulge us close,

    until many a candlemaker shall profit utmost.

MY HAPPY PLACE

Writing is my happy place,

the place I feel most secure.

Where the narrative is solely my own

and the characters betrayed are mine to hold.

To take a sliver of bare-naked thoughts

and to break down the molds entwined with plots.

Yes, writing is my happy place,

the place where I can envision a tale with grace.

TIME TO RELAX

The pressure's gone,

I feel great!

I did my job,

that's all it takes.

I'm awful tired,

so please leave me alone;

Hold all calls,

and pull the shades down.

ANGELS IN THE NIGHT

One step farther, one step higher...

As I wander into the night, I cannot see.

Which way to turn is not of my will

as now the path before me has split into two.

Angels, please be my light on this path,

help me to choose which gravel ground

to step my foot upon first,

and give me the strength not to fear

what's beyond my sight...

With you by my side, I know I'll make it

through this night.

ETERNAL FLAME

Many nights of intense passion;

A beauty marked for all,

who came to pass their judgment.

They were lovers, not a home.

They couldn't help but to have her;

Her fire burned abroad,

into the lights of stormy coves

where the messengers would call.

Call upon her beauty,

at her sensuous command;

Her breasts were sheer entrapment

for all who came in her path.

And entrapped upon her bedsheets,

they would scream and hold her tight,

then offer her forgiveness

for all her other crimes.

"Forgive me not", she would say,

with all posture in her tone.

"For I have chosen to come alive

in all sanctions, I am prone."

"But if you would like, I may,

of course, be inclined with you

and crawl into your arms tonight,

and praise that I love you!"

"But I cannot promise refuge

for your weary heart

or lie upon this bed til dawn

with your questionable heart."

"So, love me if you will,

but be sure to leave by dusk

for love's the only thing, I can only give

for a night or two at best."

So, they'd leave without a word

not a question, or a thought.

Just a kiss upon her bosom

to ensure the night's not lost.

And on that, they would go

back to their source of leave;

with the memories of the woman

who has tainted their minds eternally.

SPEAKING INTO THE CROWD

When speaking into the crowd

there is no reaction, no response.

The cues thrown up into the air to test,

do not work, the crowd just stares.

How is it one man could turn the crowd

around, but no one else who followed

could make them emanate a pulse?

How long can society cease to evolve?

The cues have landed within the fold now,

and soon a reaction will come to be,

when the man returns, speaking into the crowd.

UPON THE FOREST GREEN

Upon the Forest Green

lies a shade left unseen,

darkened by the souls of time

trapped beneath the green.

Long to walk

yet Spirits soar

lightly touched by winds of war;

Pebbles write on paper stones,

names of those lost forever.

Vultures circle high

families kneel in the aisles,

Love shuns the darkness away

if only for a while.

God bless this place where people live,

Upon the Forest Green!

MY CHRISTMAS POEM – 2022

This Christmas he will be here...

No, not with his reindeer on the roof!

But along with his angels, he will bring with him

his light, his love, and his spirit.

They will fly in a fury, as fast as speed...

No, not with a bag of toys or other

Christmas tease!

But with his light, his love, and his spirit...

They will make Christmas shine for all to see!

POETRY IS...
(EXCERPT)

...Poetry is you

written down on paper;

Poetry is life

and you it's shaper.

You guide and comfort it along the way,

you send love to the words you use every day...

CRICKETS, CRICKETS EVERYWHERE

When you finally find that one thing...that one thing that you were meant to do with your life, and you are so proud and just in awe of what you have accomplished.

But when you take that little step, to speak about it out loud, to share your happiness...all your ears can suddenly hear are crickets.

Crickets, crickets everywhere.

MY PROTECTOR

He is my protector,

he loves me and cares.

He stays and watches over me,

whenever I get scared.

He listens to what I say,

even if he can't share

the thoughts in his mind,

that need to be aired.

HUNGRY YELLOW MONSTER
(IN MY MIRROR)

The pimple on my face

is not as large as it appears...,

to others, it's just a simple speck,

from love lost along the years.

But for me,

it's the most hideous sight

ever imaginable to be seen

and it unleashes all my inner self

into a world, for which, it shall breed.

How can I attempt to stop it,

this mucus-plugged annoyance...?

before it drains my heart and soul

from all those who exclaim, "Just pop it!"

But to pop it would be to do the worst,

to do exactly as it had planned I would.

Yes, I would leave behind the scar of my life...

    For if I ever did weaken

    and place my forefingers to

    this hungry yellow monster, (in my mirror) I view,

then my life would never be mine to compare...

for my power of freedom, my choice to be true,

would never again be mine to choose.

PLAY-GROUND

Deep feelings, I have long explored,

How can the mist shed away it's lure?

The danger can be overcome

if we who choose, won't choose to run.

Let's play upon the grounded farce

and laugh until the clouds turn dark.

Then whisper softly into the dawn,

that we have chosen to remain as one.

GOLDEN NOOSE

Over the years

you've always been there.

You've been the one

who has always cared.

You spoke your mind

when I was lost...

You gave me time

when I was cross.

Even now, looking back

I am confused...

Where is this child who

you used to hold

and rock to sleep...

then run and hide

when trouble peaked?

If I could find her and bring her back,

I would...yes, I would;

But now I think she's all grown up

and reaching for the world.

So, thank you...my friend,

for staying there through night's long end,

and for holding on

when I let loose...

and for letting go

of the golden noose.

THE EYES ON THE STAIRWELL

Standing here

high above them all,

The cars,   they are whizzing by me.

I can't help but to look,

their heads are starring out

into space;   the space,

the fear of never returning...

Most are headed for an unknown place.

But I am here standing,

bright above them all,

closest to the sun – I can feel it,

beating with my pulse.

For I know something that

they do not...

there is another, who stands watch

over them today.

Sitting,   waiting silently

for their first mistakes to be made.

The profanity of the wrong turn,

evil eyes,   and sideswiping

which will lead them back

onto the correct point of their

original path. But also,

he will be made to tell true, of the nature,

of all they know,

all they will,

and all they care to...know.

For in that instant,

they will not care. Yes, they will

know of the lays before them,

but will they listen? No!

They will only become entangled

and swept away

by the excitement of the moment...

or greed of the day!

As he sits   upon the stairwell,

just one flight up from

here,   behind me,

I can feel the chill.

Although he pretends

not to look,   his eyes

often stray beyond his reading.

A little black book

with blue tainted scrolls...

Could this be his only work?

But I know for sure that

he has to be   looking,

it's in his touch.

The way his fingers turn

the pages   is known

for all who comes to peek

upon our stairwell;

Much too slow, his fingers go

that he must be looking...

somewhere else.

Somewhere beyond those

tattered pages of ink.

Yes, to breathe and beyond;

his eyes are moving now...

slowly,   from side to side.

I wonder what he knows,

how he knows, and if he...knows.

Oh no,   but wait...

If he's really not

           watching them...,

then he must be

           watching me...

Watching him!

SHATTERPROOF

She felt his presence close in on her

into her bedroom

she sensed him move

and then before she could run out to hide

he quickly sealed her passageway.

He locked the door

and then turned halfway

into the light, she saw his face

now looking through his cold green eyes

she felt him touch her

down deep inside.

She screamed for help,

but no one came

her torrid cries could not be heard

for her bedroom now

stood enclosed in glass

without a voice, she laid there still.

He made his pounce

not once or twice,

but several times as she could

count the pain

she could not move,

he had her pinned, down upon her own

private bed.

Now when he was through,

he just got up,

and looked upon her ragged state

then shook his head, as in disgrace,

and left the room just as he came.

Her screams, now turned to whimpers,

embraced her pillow's case

and now clinging to her bed with fright

her cries masturbated themselves

into the night.

THE RIVER'S END

Bearing down on a quarter inch of your soul,

a salty taste...your tongue now holds;

And you eclipsed beyond a fault to charge

cannot bring yourself to denounce the barge.

With every ring, your heart stands still to scope,

the water's rage...with Fall's tempest gate.

Churning now, your fate has been long since sealed,

with all your packaged charms sent home to waste.

As the swimmers of this school commence

to listen once more how their tails are strung;

When given the choice, the chance to kneel or bend...

Why haven't you yet found the river's end?

WORDS

When words never quite seem

to make sense,

yet somehow as time permits,

they fall silently into place.

When you think of someone

who's been hurt,

can't image them ever being the same,

hold tight those words ...

help to heal the pain.

THROUGH A POET'S EYES
(VERSION 1)

If only once...I could make him see

a world of beauty, induced by gleam;

where shadows come only when ill is near,

and the puppies play, as all becomes clear.

For daylight only speaks it's will

when his eyes alone, are proud and full.

The tears of laxity shall make it known,

that the world has troubles, not him alone.

And as hopeful as I shall caress

I'm afraid too long, has made its path;

Across Beach Road, Bridge Street is home.

Shall we jump together, or move on and grow?

If only once...my tongue could convey

all that would be missed if he was to go away.

Maybe then, these words could vent some reality

upon the choice to leave, and the choice to stay.

THROUGH A POET'S EYES
(VERSION 2)

If only once...I could make him see

a world of beauty, induced by gleam;

where shadows come only when ill is near,

and the puppies play, as all becomes clear.

For daylight only speaks it's will

when his eyes alone, are proud and full.

The tears of freedom shall make it known,

that the world has troubles, not him alone.

And as hopeful as I shall embrace

I'm afraid too long, has made its way;

Across Beach Road, Bridge Street is home.

Shall we jump together, or move on and grow?

If only once...my tongue could learn to speak

but my hands won't allow it, to face the dream.

So, as the written word is my last chance to find

the light of hope, through a poet's eyes.

THE HOMESTEAD

Blueberry bushes

and blackberry too,

surrounded the house

in full bloom.

Maple trees

and a small round swing,

gave beauty to the home

in the midst of spring.

Old wooden shutters,

rusty nails and bolts,

brought out special traits

of this little wooden house.

The homestead we call it,

with all the beauty it deserves;

Filled with memories and love

of six generations served.

BUTTERFLIES ARE PRETTY

I have no clue what this poem is about

the words are not coming out tonight.

    Maybe I'm forcing it?

    Maybe it's not the right time?

But let's see what happens

as I continue to write.

Butterflies are pretty

The ocean is blue

I like how the big birds swoop down

and pick out their food.

Poor fishes...no chance had they

once they were spotted along the ocean's bay.

Butterflies are pretty

I like puppy dogs too!

I remember chasing with mine

around the house all summer afternoon,

then lying on the couch, tucked in each other's arms,

loving as a whole, and belonging to someone's heart.

Butterflies are pretty

Yes, I think I've said that before,

but as I don't know where this is going,

I'm just going to keep saying it some more.

Butterflies are pretty

Roses are lovely too…

The red and pink ones are my favorites,

but I've never understood

why they have to have thorns!

Butterflies are pretty

All their colors shaped in scheme

a magnifying rainbow netted into wings

And when they perch upon a group of buds

sitting by a stream –

The sun entraps the prism-bow and glorifies the scene.

Butterflies are pretty

Oh, I'm so glad that you're still here!

Writing something when there's nothing

is somewhat difficult to do –

    Yet, Butterflies are pretty

    no matter how a verse shapes in form

And I do hope you enjoyed reading – my little poem.

THE VALLEY OF LOVE

In the valley of love

there lie many closed doors,

each one to be opened by another.

He who holds the key

also holds a spare,

one to unlock the door

and one to open your heart.

    Is he the one you've been looking for?

    Waiting for?

    Longing for?

    Like a lost treasure in the snow,

    searching high and low for?

Come now and unlock my door

steal my heart

take away my treasures...

If you are truly the one

it shalt not matter.

Come now

into the valley of love.

MISS KITTY

Green eyes peer through my window

with coats of gray and white –

shimmering through the sun streams.

Could this be God's solemn plight?

Enticed with all her beauty

she sits, as like the angels sing;

patience and restrain have bestowed her

with the voice of many muted Kings.

How can she be with master?

Can I ever truly call her, to mine?

With name and collar, is it proper

to hold such a spirit down?

But whether she sings of mishaps,

or the beautified heavens above,

it will never be clear, for which, she has come

until I have welcomed her in.

WHO KNOWS

Who knows not what I did before

or who I used to be...

Who knows not,

for I hardly remember myself...

as now, I lie here covered in fleece.

In distant times, on distant shores

you may not remember thee...

But I do know that,

you will come to stand for everything,

I too have longed believed.

I see myself as ever I shall

tied down upon this place, for which,

I do not care to dwell...

My children, they will come,

not knowing of my fate

and they will suffer the affliction

for the crimes, for which, I am plagued.

But somehow they will run away,

and find themselves a new ground for stay,

with hopes, only I could have wished them blessed

and with no curse upon them...

as the cross upon myself.

It is now the time,

too late to gallop,

against the offshore tide;

the soldiers are coming...

the soldiers are coming...

And now I must lay to die.

THE TALLEST MAN
(EXCERPT)

...I remember all the walks

from the homestead into town

and of how he wore the biggest shoes...

of all the men in town.

And the pats upon our shoulders

every now and then,

meant more to me than anything...

but I didn't know it then.

MADELEINE
(EXCERPT)

...You have passed onto me the gift to learn,

and the right to claim my own free verse.

But above all, you have bestowed upon me...

the strength to stand on my own two feet!

BENEATH THE APRIL SHOWERS

Beneath the April showers sprang

the freshest breath he'd ever smelt;

The kindest air, or breeze, blew by...

as if it knew, he had needed strength.

The strength, to sing goodbye aloud

beneath the April showers song;

But she had to leave him, and that was wrong.

Beneath the April showers long;

Her words, had struck him, too close to lie

(a touch of numbness, ran through his mind).

But with his longing to sing in tune

and to breathe, at first, without the moon;

Who's moonlit arms had snuggled close...

Before the April showers met.

He had found the strength to stay anew

Beneath the April showers left...himself.

FOR EMILY

My beautiful sunshine

My heart, my love

You have no idea how much you truly mean to me

or how much I would truly be lost without ever having

you.

My center took a lovely curve

the morning you were born — a baby girl

who brought a shower of flowers, colors, and lacey things

into my world.

Oh, how much I miss your baby curls!

As you explore, as young adults do –

college, friendships, more than friendships..., and life's

goals,

I hope you will find your own course to walk –

the strength to go further, and the patience to endure

anything that may block your path.

As your Granny would say, "Chin up, shoulders back..." –

You can do anything you set your mind to do.

I love you, my dear Emily...with all my heart!

ONE MAN

One man –

He heard me when no one else did

He heard my words,

even though others forbid

No allowance of time,

not a second was fair –

My words were not permitted

to speak into the air

    And yet he heard me

    amidst all the noise

    And he listened,

    and he answered

    without judging my voice.

The others were angered,

for my thoughts were not of theirs

But that wasn't a concern for this man –

For he had dealt with "the others"

in different places and times

and there wasn't one that could sway him

to believe in their babbling of rhymes.

He chose to believe in living

for his dream and for his heart –

And it is to this one man

that I am forever grateful...

For letting me share my thoughts.

PERCHED

I see...flood lights down the driveway

5 frogs perched upon the brick wall

The fireflies are stunning in the darkness...

I do hope they make it past the frogs!

I see...an owl perched on the tree branch across the street

A mouse scurrying along the walkway

And there's Chester, our kitty cat, perched - eyeing the

mouse's tail, with a grin...

I do hope that owl stays across the street!

I see...a long black snake coiled up against my porch

2 baby opossums playing under my azalea bush

Oops, they woke up the snake...he's moving in their way...

I see...the owl fly from across the street —

Bye-bye Mr. Snake!

A FOLKLORE TALE

Twas this what fate had imagined to be

to hath create this folklore-ish tale?

Entwined with imagery of fire and ghoul

Two hearts of different worlds — to share a space?

In theory, maybe a stage could be seen

far off to the distance, one eye might see,

but then steady the hand of treble by tune

and another eye might just glimpse a duel.

Conducting in simultaneous vibe, is uncertain at best

but as these two Spirits were viewed, one eye could attest -

Whether by the goodness from above, or the sinful realm underneath,

even through the murkiest of nights, one single star always peeked.

As entertainment goes, they did put on quite a show.

Musically, the Starman and the Demon — complete in fold,

But watch out, the eyes have seen and forewarned

there's a mystical side that works here — as this tale will be told.

Was their stage created for darkness?

Attention?

Or perhaps just a glare?

Could deception lie in the mist for the mass parades

that would circle the stage on the Royal's chosen days?

What a spectacle these two showmen would create.

Could it be that this was all just a mere facade?

The Starman, truly an attraction by himself to be seen —

with an instrumental voice that would call the lasses, as he pleased.

The Demon, with axe bass — climbs bare from the pit,

as darkness covers all — the night is his to be seized.

Yes, with black diamond eyes, and a blood-ish dagger tongue,

one would think the Demon would command —

But to hath, one may think wrong.

For you see,

The Starman's prose was not fit to be teased

His voice set the stage in a magnificent key

And on occasion he was known,

yes — one eye might actually see...

his voice command the Demon — to drop to his knees.

This is not to say the Demon did not have his way

on occasion, he too, would not let **A Star** in his way.

The eyes, still quite a dazed, will never forget the day...

    As he pointed his torch in line with his feud,

    and blew a blaze of fire - stage left of his view,

and as the eyes will swear...

The blaze struck the Starman straight in his derriere!

Only two hearts, as brothers, could deliver such blows.

As the facade continued, night after fateful night...

one wondered if it was all for show?

In truth, could it be that these duelists were actually

brothers...indeed?

One eye believed so, one eye shook in disbelief – No!

To entrance their parades into believing in a tale

then to have it all unravel that fateful night...

When the stage lights suddenly peaked to a glow

   and then the parades witnessed

   the Demon's sly smirk to his foe

   and the Starry wink that was quickly returned – Oh yes, both

the Demon and the Starman seemed quite pleased with the show!

As some parades grew in fury that night, when truth be shown

the Starman and the Demon eyed each other an unhappy tone –

And summoning a bolt of lightning as the final song was to be played,

the brothers vanished, where as they stood – and the stage went up

in flames.

ABOUT THE AUTHOR

Maureen Himler lives in Columbia, South Carolina with her three wonderful young people, Erich, Emily, and Christopher. She enjoys writing poetry and children's stories, shopping at thrift stores, attending concerts and conventions, and spending time with her Golden Retriever, Mae. In August 2015, she published her first children's book "Princess Emily and the Terrible Itch!". Maureen currently has her own line of tote bags and other products which feature her poetry on them. Please visit https://simplymopoetry.square.site to view her products.